The Piano Works of
RACHMANINOFF

RUSSIAN RHAPSODY

Two Pianos/Four Hands

Edited by
MAURICE HINSON

PREFACE

The **Russian Rhapsody** is an original work for two pianos composed between January 12-14, 1891 when Rachmaninoff was 18 years old. A planned performance by Rachmaninoff and his fellow-student L. Maksimov, at a student concert at the Moscow Conservatory on February 24, 1891, did not take place. The work was played there however on October 17, 1891 by Rachmaninoff and Josef Lhevinne. Alexander Goldenweiser recalled the first performance:

> Someone had told him that nothing could be written on a certain Russian theme. He wrote a composition in E minor (in the form of variations). It was quite good music. I remember that at some benefit concert for our colleagues—we often arranged such concerts—Rachmaninoff and Lhevinne performed this piece on two pianos; it concluded with a variation in octaves, alternating from one pianist to the other, and on that occasion each increased the tempo, and everyone watched to see who would outplay whom. Each had a phenomenal wrist, but it was Rachmaninoff who won[1].

This work is apparently one of the first of Rachmaninoff's instrumental works to use a Russian theme as its basis. It is not a sequence of folk tunes but a set of variations on a Russian folk theme. Vivid and brilliant writing are reminiscent of Liszt's **Hungarian Fantasia.**

The original manuscript of **Russian Rhapsody** is located in the Central Museum in Moscow. It consists of 40 pages of music of 12 lines each written in ink. The two movements are: Moderato—Vivace—Meno mosso (in E minor), and Andante—Con moto (G major).

Playing time of the piece is approximately 8½ minutes.

Maurice Hinson

[1]Sergei Bertennson, Jay Leyda. **Sergei Rachmaninoff. A Lifetime in Music.. New York University Press, 1956, p. 41.**

RUSSIAN RHAPSODY
(1891)

I.

SERGEI RACHMANINOFF
EDITED BY MAURICE HINSON

EL03607

II.

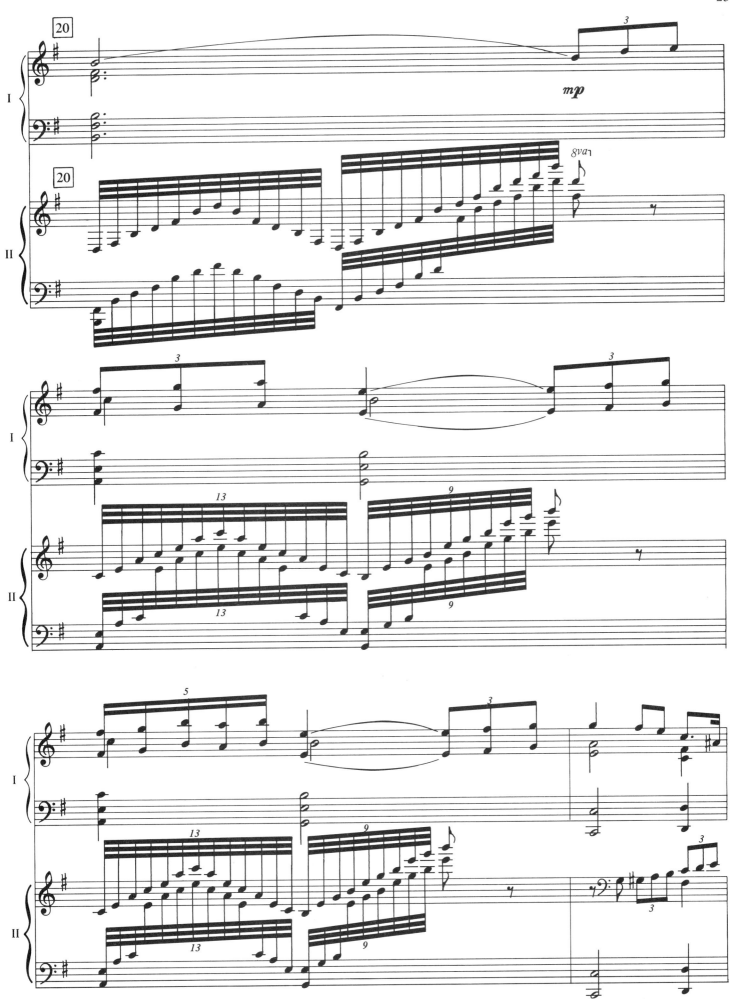